Working Paper Series

New Yardsticks to Measure Financial Distress

By Kent John Chabotar
Vice President for Finance and Administration and Treasurer,
Bowdoin College

and

James P. Honan
Associate Director of Programs in Professional Education and
Lecturer, Harvard Graduate School of Education

INQUIRY #4

NEW PATHWAYS: FACULTY CAREERS AND EMPLOYMENT FOR THE 21ST CENTURY

A PROJECT OF THE AMERICAN ASSOCIATION FOR HIGHER EDUCATION

About the Authors

Kent John Chabotar has been vice president for finance and administration and treasurer and senior lecturer on government at Bowdoin College since 1991. Previously, he held faculty and administrative positions at the Harvard Graduate School of Education, University of Massachusetts at Boston, and Michigan State University. His other publications include "Managing Participative Budgeting in Higher Education" and "Coping With Retrenchment" (with James Honan), both in *Change,* and "Financial Ratio Analysis Comes to Nonprofits" in the *Journal of Higher Education.* Chabotar received M.P.A. and Ph.D. degrees in public administration from the Maxwell School at Syracuse University.

James P. Honan is associate director of programs in professional education and lecturer on education at the Harvard Graduate School of Education. He is educational chair of the Institute for Educational Management and of the Management Development Program. Previously, he served as institutional research coordinator in the Office of Budgets at Harvard University and project analyst in Harvard's University Financial Aid Office. He holds a B.A. from Marist College, an M.A. and Ed.S. in higher education from George Washington University, and an Ed.M. and Ed.D. in administration, planning, and social policy from Harvard University.

About the New Pathways Working Paper Series

The Forum on Faculty Roles & Rewards is a special program of the American Association for Higher Education (AAHE). It works with faculty leaders, senior academic administrators, trustees, legislators, and others interested in refocusing faculty priorities to address pressing institutional and societal needs. To advance this agenda, AAHE initiated a project called "New Pathways: Faculty Careers and Employment for the 21st Century." The New Pathways Working Paper Series addresses key issues related to changing faculty careers and employment arrangements; the series consists of 14 papers.

The American Association for Higher Education is a national, individual-membership organization that brings people together — across hierarchies, sectors, and disciplines — in the common cause of improving the quality of higher education.

Ordering Information

Additional copies of this Inquiry or others in the fourteen-Inquiry Working Paper Series can be purchased from:
American Association for Higher Education
One Dupont Circle, Suite 360
Washington, DC 20036-1110
202/293-6440, fax 202/293-0073, pubs@aahe.org
www.aahe.org

Reprint Permission

AAHE's New Pathways project has as one of its missions to disseminate information and foster discussion. With that purpose in mind, AAHE grants to the purchaser of this Working Paper permission to photocopy and distribute it.

Design by Kerrie Kemperman

FOREWORD

In 1992, AAHE entered into the growing national debate about the priorities of the professoriate by establishing the Forum on Faculty Roles & Rewards — a program that sponsors an annual national conference, issues publications, and serves as a general clearinghouse. Thus, when tenure surfaced in the spring of 1994 as a major issue of conversation and media attention, we became an interested party in the discussion.

On reflection, we decided that what was needed was not another familiar debate about the pros and cons of tenure but a new dialogue — a dialogue in which tenure was placed in a larger context of fresh thinking about two questions: What career paths make sense for the professoriate of the 21st century? What varieties of employment arrangements might most appropriately undergird these paths?

We also concluded that what might best help campuses work through these questions was not more philosophical argument but concrete options: practical ideas about new career paths and imaginative employment arrangements that campuses could try on for size.

AAHE's New Pathways project seeks to carry out that agenda. Project activities include (1) sponsoring forums to advance the dialogue; (2) serving as a general clearinghouse; and (3) initiating investigations into selected, particular issues.

Central direction for the project is provided by a three-person team: R. Eugene Rice, director of AAHE's Forum on Faculty Roles & Rewards; Richard Chait, professor of higher education, Harvard Graduate School of Education; and Judith Gappa, professor and vice president for human relations at Purdue University. Richard Chait's part of the project, which focuses on creative employment arrangements, is supported by a generous grant from the Pew Charitable Trusts.

The project team in turn benefits from the wise counsel of a four-person national advisory panel: Richard Lyman, president emeritus, Stanford University (chair); Andrew Hurwitz, attorney; Ejner Jensen, professor of English and special counsel to the president, University of Michigan; and Linda Wilson, president, Radcliffe College.

We wanted to make our own investigations quickly available in a form that was affordable, easily duplicated, and suggestive of what they really are: works in progress, intended to stimulate and enrich further discussion.

Russell Edgerton

President, American Association for Higher Education

New Yardsticks
To Measure Financial Distress [*]

by Kent John Chabotar and James P. Honan

▶ In 1994, prompted by a 28 percent drop in enrollment over ten years and an annual revenue shortfall of $2 million, Bennington College dismissed twenty-two faculty members (28 percent of the total). Many had been at Bennington for decades and had "presumptive tenure." The college also slashed tuition by 10 percent and eliminated all academic departments (Dembner, 1994:21).

▶ In February 1994, the executive committee of its Board of Trustees declared a financial crisis at St. Bonaventure University. Chronic budget deficits totaled almost $10 million between FY 1990-91 and FY 1993-94. Undergraduate enrollment had dropped 24 percent in five years. That May, eighteen tenured faculty members received notice of termination. Other actions included a 6.5 percent reduction in employee salaries and cuts in the university's contributions to retirement and health care premiums (Zekan, 1995).

▶ Maryland's Essex Community College was ordered by a Baltimore County judge to reinstate two tenured professors as of July 1994, calling the handling of their firings a "travesty of justice." According to the judge, the college had no complaints about the abilities of the professors, only an after-the-fact claim that the college had money problems (Lyons, 1995:3B).

▶ In response to a possible reduction in state funding of more than 10 percent, the trustees of the City University of New York voted in March 1996 to declare a state of financial exigency. The presidents of each of CUNY's senior colleges formed retrenchment committees to recommend

---

[*]The authors gratefully acknowledge the advice and assistance of Richard Chait, Robert Culver, Robert Edwards, Donald Heller, Steven Jacques, Bruce Johnstone, Cathy Trower, and Gordon Winston.

---

faculty and program cuts for their campuses. The declaration of financial exigency, CUNY's second in as many years, allowed the university to lay off tenured faculty with twelve months' notice (Arenson, 1996:B1,B5).

The past two decades have been a period of great stress in the American economy, and no less so in higher education. At the start of this "time of troubles," institutions balanced their budgets mainly by hiking tuition at twice the rate of inflation and increasing endowment use, especially in private institutions. Some institutions deferred maintenance or sold assets to make ends meet. As higher education's crisis lingered and these obvious actions had been taken, colleges and universities also began cutting administrative and support positions and expense budgets. After all, that was where most of the growth had occurred; the number of college administrators had soared by 60 percent between 1975 and 1985 (Zemsky and Massy, 1990:22), a period in which faculty numbers increased by 6 percent (Waggaman, 1991:40). "Cut the fat" was an expression applied primarily to administrators and support staff. Full-time and especially tenured faculty were spared in order to preserve the academic mission.

But, that is no longer true. Higher education's financial problems have become so persistent and pervasive that many institutions are running out of options to balance their budgets. That economic reality is compounded by unfortunate public perceptions about higher education . . . that a college education costs too much . . . that tenure protects unproductive teachers . . . that in a rapidly changing world, faculty have been slow to innovate. All these factors have pressured institutions to put layoffs of faculty, including *tenured* faculty, "in play" as a way to restore financial equilibrium.

Purpose of This Paper

That about two-thirds of faculty hold tenure (NCES, 1993:227, 239) makes it very hard to consider large-scale faculty dismissals as a viable solution to budgetary problems. Legislators and trustees, intent on cutting costs in tough economic times, are frustrated with having to meet uncompromising or unclear standards of financial exigency before layoffs of tenured faculty are allowed. In their frustration, they are increasingly calling for tenure to be amended, abolished, or replaced with long-term contracts. (Ironically, the very policies that were designed to protect tenure are, in their inflexibility and ambiguousness, threatening tenure's existence.)

In this paper, we come neither to praise nor to bury faculty tenure. In fact, we presume that tenure will continue indefinitely in its present form at many institutions. We also do not enter the argument about whether financial problems and tenure *should* be linked; all that matters is that, increasingly, they are. We acknowledge that institutions and programs in financial trouble will and should try to raise revenue and cut costs in other ways (Chabotar and Honan, 1990) before turning to dismissing faculty. Finally, we do not advocate a particular decision-making process: *who* should decide when a financial crisis exists that would affect faculty with tenure, or *how* to choose which faculty should be dismissed. Roles of governance committees, provisions for dislocated faculty, and other procedural issues are beyond the scope of this paper, as are "last hired, first fired" and alternative criteria for layoffs.

Instead, our purpose is much narrower but ultimately more important. *What do "financial emergency," "exigency," and similar terms mean, if they are going to be used as grounds to legitimate layoffs of tenured faculty?* Our intent is to prompt institutions to reduce subjective judgments in favor of clear and operational definitions, agreed upon in advance, then implemented when the situation warrants.

We contend that most of the generally accepted definitions of financial distress lack the specificity needed to guide academic policy or administrative action about the termination of tenured faculty. Fuzzy yardsticks contribute to uncertainty and inconsistency, suspicions of inequity and politics, and delay in responding to financial distress.

It is not our aim to advocate a particular approach or definition, but rather to proliferate options and analyze the trade-offs that each of these alternatives poses. That a college or university has a clear, working definition of financial distress for the institution as well as for its individual programs matters more than precisely what that definition is. As Saunders (1984:43) contends:

> There is no single ideal model for all financial exigency policies. Some variation will be inevitable. Each policy must be tailored to the unique characteristics of the institution for which it is intended: financial exigency policy must reflect the mission, philosophies, and needs of the college or university that implements it.

Preview

What lies ahead? In this paper we provide general principles that should underlie all criteria and standards of financial exigency, e.g., they should be established before a crisis hits, and data almost always evaluated over more than a single year. We then analyze specific yardsticks within three broad categories of indicators of financial condition:

- operating results (budget, cash flow, and student enrollment)
- net worth
- bond ratings.

Operating results apply to both institution-wide and program-based decisions, whereas net worth and bond ratings are more relevant to the institution as a whole.

Next, we suggest two alternatives to traditional accounting methods that have the potential to strengthen the comprehensiveness and credibility of an institution's financial data: "global accounts" and new accounting standards from the Financial Accounting Standards Board. Finally, we summarize the advantages and limitations of alternative yardsticks. We also advance a hypothetical definition of exigency that exemplifies the sort of clarity and specificity that we believe institutions need in order to dismiss tenured faculty during a financial crisis.

CURRENT DEFINITIONS OF FINANCIAL EXIGENCY

Most colleges and universities already have "financial exigency" and similar clauses in their faculty handbooks and union contracts to provide a process and a rationale for dismissing tenured faculty under such conditions. But do they also provide a reasonable definition of what constitutes a financial exigency?

AAUP Definition

The American Association of University Professors (AAUP) drafted the most frequently cited definition. In its *Recommended Institutional Regulations on Academic Freedom and Tenure* (1982:23), the AAUP states:

> Termination of an appointment with continuous tenure . . . may occur under extraordinary circumstances because of a demonstrably *bona fide* financial exigency, i.e.,

> *an imminent financial crisis which threatens the survival of the institution as a whole and which cannot be alleviated by less drastic means* [emphasis added].

Strictly speaking, this definition is legally binding only at institutions that have specifically incorporated the AAUP's guidelines in their faculty handbooks or collective bargaining agreements.

Overall, about a third of the faculty workforce, public and private, is unionized (Douglas, 1990). Gary Rhoades, of the University of Arizona, studied the retrenchment clauses of forty-two contracts negotiated in the 1980s by the AAUP as well as the American Federation of Teachers and the National Education Association (1993:324-325,327). Financial exigency was mentioned as a condition justifying retrenchment in eighteen of the contracts, or about 40 percent. It was far more frequently mentioned at four-year than at two-year institutions. Interestingly, the AAUP definition of financial exigency as a crisis that "threatens . . . the institution as a whole" was cited in only three contracts. This suggests that, in some instances, program discontinuance and the dismissal of tenured faculty might occur in situations where specific programs are deemed not to be financially viable. [While the AAUP recognizes that tenured faculty may be dismissed when a program or department is eliminated, it feels dismissal should be "based essentially upon educational considerations . . . [that] reflect long-range judgments that the educational mission of the institution as a whole will be enhanced by the discontinuance" (AAUP, 1982:25).] For example, Rhoades (1993:323-324) cites two state university systems where faculty contracts linked retrenchment with "program curtailment, elimination of courses" (Pennsylvania) and "reorganization of degree or curriculum offerings or requirements . . . or curtailment of one or more programs or functions" (New York).

Nevertheless, the AAUP's interpretation has been mentioned so often that it has become, at some colleges and universities and in some courts, the academic equivalent of common law in dealing with layoffs of tenured faculty. Its advocates claim that tenure has protected academic freedom and creativity among faculty, leading to a system of higher education in the United States that is the best in the world. Thus, "the general community of higher education has joined the AAUP in recognizing that involuntary termination of a faculty appointment carrying continuous tenure on financial grounds . . . should be an exceptional action in the life of an institution, to be taken only under exacting criteria" (Kreiser, 1985:61).

Others assert that the AAUP definition is ambiguous. What precisely is meant by "extraordinary circumstances," "a demonstrably *bona fide* financial exigency," or "an imminent financial crisis"? The definition may also be unrealistic by mandating, in effect, that an entire institution, not merely a specific program or unit, be on the precipice of bankruptcy before tenured faculty can be terminated. A lower court judge in the 1978 case of *Krotkoff v. Goucher College* opined that in defining financial exigency:

> It does not mean that you have to be walking down to the clerk's office with a bankruptcy petition in your pocket . . . but it means that if things keep going the way they are going, you are going to be in trouble pretty soon and maybe out of business (Weeks, 1980:36).

Other Definitions

Many colleges and universities have definitions of financial exigency that are also somewhat inexact. For example:

> an imminent and substantial deficiency in available University financial resources which warrants reduction or elimination of University programs. (University of Wyoming, 1993:1)

> critical, pressing or urgent need of the College to reorder its monetary expenditures in such a way as to remedy and relieve the state of urgency within the College created by its inability to meet its annual monetary expenditures with sufficient revenue to prevent a sustained loss of funds (Colby-Sawyer College, 1995:35).

Rhoades's study found that of the contracts that did not mention financial exigency, five referred in some way to financial conditions as a rationale for cutting faculty positions. He concluded that terms such as "insufficient funds," "economic considerations," and "reduction of funds" lacked specificity and "implied that retrenchment was justified even when problems fell far short of a crisis" (1993:328).

The suspicion, shared by the AAUP, is that institutions will use a temporary or modest fiscal shortfall as an excuse to remove troublesome tenured faculty or to reorganize schools and programs. In a draft of campus policies on dismissal of tenured faculty, Indiana University Purdue University Indianapolis (IUPUI, 1995:1-2) distinguishes between *true* financial exigency and two other situations. These latter situations would not involve financial exigency and thus not threaten "the imminent dismissal of tenured faculty or librarians":

> Temporary Adjustments
> First, it is expected that financial problems will occur from time to time, and these ordinarily will not require lasting changes in programs or the elimination of tenured faculty . . . The degree program and the operational unit itself may change but remain intact. In such cases, temporary changes in operation may be made which will permit the affected program to recover.

> Permanent Adjustments
> Secondly, it is expected that academic institutions will change in the course of time,

resulting in the formation of new schools . . . as well as the dissolution, merger, or transfer of existing schools . . . In such cases, the creation of new or the transformation of existing units is expected to occur according to a plan which will NOT require the dismissal of tenured faculty . . . even if they are relocated and retrained.

CRITERIA AND STANDARDS OF FINANCIAL DISTRESS

Fundamentally, definitions of financial distress can be viewed as reflecting annual operating results, net worth, or both. Always, qualitative performance *criteria* must be distinguished from quantitative performance *standards*. For example, a college may select "revenue per student" as a criterion, but further specify "drops to $25,000 per student" or "declines by 3 percent per year for three years" as the standard to precipitate declaration of a financial emergency. Both criteria and standards are needed for an adequate definition.

All criteria and standards should be *defined ahead of* any crisis. Otherwise, once the crisis has hit, all sides will argue indefinitely and tailor their arguments to fit their biases and the existing facts. An institution's response to a financial exigency may be *carried out in stages:* Certain indicators might trigger selective layoffs, for example, while other indicators might prompt those layoffs to quicken or expand. Trigger conditions should require historical data *evaluated over a period of time*, at least three to five years if possible; temporary fluctuations could lead to premature action. But, this does not mean that an institution has to wait years in every case before responding. Further, the situation today should be *projected* to detect whether improvements are likely and in sufficient time to avoid a crisis.

It is also important for the institution to define whether the criteria and standards must be applied *institution-wide* or only to a *particular program or unit*. For example, if the university as a whole has stable enrollments but the school of education is losing students, is it permissible to declare an emergency only in that school? Finally, the credibility of the analysis will be strengthened to the extent that a declaration of financial exigency depends on *multiple criteria and standards*.

Operating Results

The three principal indicators of negative operating results in higher education are budget deficits, cash flow problems, and drops in student enrollment.

Budget Deficits

One measure of operating results that might lead to layoffs of tenured faculty is a deficit in the annual operating budget. Under the conventions of fund accounting, this usually means a budget deficit in the operating fund, better known as the "current fund." (Some public institutions use the term "general fund.") Fund accounting is a practice used throughout higher education and other nonprofit organizations to distinguish among types of resources, including *current* funds for salaries, the operations of auxiliary enterprises such as dining services and the bookstore, and other operating expenditures such as laboratory equipment and faculty travel; *plant* funds for buildings, equipment, and other capital assets; and *endowment* funds.

Two possible criteria for financial exigency can be expressed in terms of ratios:

1.　　Negative net change in current fund balance as a percentage of total revenue. This is the accounting equivalent of a budget deficit. The calculation includes all sources and uses of current funds, including "restricted" revenues for financial aid and other donor-imposed purposes. The net change in fund balance is the numerical result of deducting total expenditures and mandatory interfund transfers from total revenue. (There are two types of interfund transfers of money between funds: mandatory to meet contractual and legal obligations, and nonmandatory at the discretion of the board for purposes such as creating reserves in the endowment or plant funds. In this case, only mandatory transfers from the current fund to other funds are added to operating expenditures to calculate total spending.) A negative net change means you have brought in less than you spent, and so have drawn down the fund balance.

Secondary ratios might consider educational and general (E&G) activities — such as instruction and research — separately from auxiliary enterprises, but the primary ratio should be inclusive of all institutional resources if financial viability and layoffs of tenured faculty are being considered.

M.S. Richards (1991 as cited in Rhoades, 1993:321) provides examples of what the courts have found to be budget deficits sufficient to declare financial exigency, even when mismanagement contributed to the problem. These included both criteria and occasional standards:

> (1) where the legislature did not appropriate a budget large enough to continue the same number of faculty positions; (2) where the legislature mandated a 2.5 percent budget reduction for the next fiscal year and enrollments were reduced; (3) where a school had an operating deficit for six years and anticipated another deficit year after having adopted remedial measures; and (4) where a school experienced six years of deficits, diminishing endowments, and declining enrollment.

For example, the University of Washington prepared to declare a financial emergency in 1991 after a state revenue shortfall caused the governor to order a 10 percent budget cut of $32 million. While specific plans were being developed to eliminate programs and tenured faculty, the legislature reduced the university's cut to 5.5 percent, which the administration found manageable. The financial emergency was rescinded (NACUBO, 1992:5-6).

2.   <u>Negative net change in unrestricted current fund balance as a percentage of total revenue.</u> This criterion focuses *only* on unrestricted revenues, expenditures, and mandatory transfers. These resources are far more available to cope with emergencies than are funds restricted to faculty chairs, student financial aid, and other restricted or board-designated purposes.

With respect to standards, sporadic small operating deficits are often no cause for alarm, and neither is a large deficit in any one year if sufficient reserves exist in endowment and similar funds to cover it. Chabotar (1989:199) suggests that most nonprofit organizations would be disturbed if they discovered an operating fund deficit: (1) for two consecutive years; (2) greater than the previous year's; (3) in two or more of the last five years; or (4) equaling more than 10 percent of total revenue. IUPUI's draft policies on dismissal of tenured faculty (1995:4) link financial exigency with operating deficits:

> Due to the complexity of the IUPUI campus and its many different units, no single criterion or guideline can be stated which would anticipate all of the possible conditions which might evoke consideration of financial exigency. However, an unplanned, one-year deficit of 3% (i.e., the equivalent of the unit's income shortfall reserve) might be sufficient to warrant planning for action under financial exigency provisions.

The advantage of the operating deficit as a criterion for financial exigency is that it is already a broadly understood and widely used definition of fiscal distress. Training in accounting is not required to grasp the concept. From the proposed constitutional amendment to compel a balanced federal budget, to reported budget deficits at the University of California and even Harvard, examples of the causes and consequences of persistent operating deficits abound. Chronic deficits mean persons and positions are eliminated, programs and services closed, and new revenues are desperately sought. Budget deficits are also as relevant to program or unit financial crises as they are to an entire college or university. A $900,000 operating deficit prompted Harvard's Graduate School of Design to terminate 20 percent of its office staff and drop its evening program (Chabotar and Honan, 1990:30).

A limitation of using operating budget deficits to legitimate faculty layoffs is that the institution may have endowment or other resources that could be used to avert a crisis. In 1989, Johns Hopkins announced a 10 percent reduction of its arts and sciences faculty after a $7 million operating deficit, despite a capital campaign that had already raised $500 million (Chabotar and Honan, 1990:33). If a university has chronic budget deficits but can access, for example, a substantial endowment, does it have a true financial emergency? Unrestricted "quasi-endowment" funds would be easiest to tap; these comprise budget surpluses and gifts saved from prior years that can be spent in their entirety (principal, capital gains, and income) for whatever purpose the governing board decides. The criteria in such a situation might be a budget deficit *and* spending from the endowment equivalent to a large percentage of the endowment's market value. The standard for a "large" percentage might, in turn, be when the percentage return on investment, less the percentage spent, less the inflation rate is less than zero. For example, if the university's endowment was earning 10 percent on invested assets, of which the university was spending 8 percent, and inflation was 4 percent, this would meet such a standard for a financial exigency (10% – 8% – 4% = –2%). Another standard might be real declines in total endowment market value — including return on invested assets and new gifts — after adjusting for inflation; a college whose endowment grew only 2 percent in a year of 4 percent inflation would qualify here.

> IF A UNIVERSITY HAS CHRONIC BUDGET DEFICITS BUT CAN ACCESS, FOR EXAMPLE, A SUBSTANTIAL ENDOWMENT, DOES IT HAVE A TRUE FINANCIAL EMERGENCY?

Yet, institutions should not be compelled to have "fire sales" of capital assets such as land, buildings, or stocks/bonds to buttress their operating budgets and avoid financial exigency. For example, despite an endowment approaching $1.3 billion, Washington University announced it was shutting down its sociology department, after having previously closed its dental school (Chabotar and Honan 1990:30). In reviewing relevant court cases, both Weeks (1980:36) and Rhoades (1993:321) conclude that financial exigency sufficient to lay off tenured faculty referred to a college or university's operating funds and not to its capital assets. This is a well-established principle of case law on higher education (Houpt, 1991:7).

Another limitation of using deficits as a criterion is that current fund deficits can be orchestrated. An institution can exacerbate its deficit by shifting revenues and expenses from one fiscal year into another year. Under fund accounting, colleges and other nonprofits can create or obscure deficits in the current fund by interfund borrowing or nonmandatory transfers for perfectly legitimate reasons.

For example, Bowdoin College aimed at a balanced current fund budget in three years while reducing tuition increases and endowment spending (Chabotar, 1995:22). Due to unexpectedly high enrollment and endowment growth, and accelerated staffing reductions, the deficit could have been eliminated after two years. However, the pressures to limit revenues from higher tuition and the endowment and to control costs would have abated if the college had declared early "victory" in the budget battle. More important, the College would have been left with no plant or operating reserves, which had been depleted to cover past deficits, and a seriously under funded pension plan. Thus, the administration made several nonmandatory transfers from the current fund to these other funds to meet their needs. These transfers perpetuated an apparent current fund deficit in year 2.

Faculty and others fear that such financial flexibility can also be used by an institution to "invent" an operating deficit that would allow it to dismiss tenured faculty. Gordon Winston, of Williams College, cautions against using any criteria for financial exigency that might be "gamed — manipulated by an administration to create a fake crisis in order to suspend tenure" (1995). One safeguard would be to exclude nonmandatory transfers from any calculation of total expenditures when figuring the deficit or surplus for the year.

Cash Flow Problems

Colleges and universities may have severe cash flow problems (be unable to pay their bills with the cash then available) despite a balanced budget. Meeting payroll and other short-term expenses can be a challenge when an institution depends on two or three revenue surges each year when tuition bills are paid. An institution may have adequate revenues for the year but not during critical periods when bills are due. Inadequate cash flow threatens the survival of many small colleges almost as much as an unbalanced budget.

Private institutions with small endowments from which surplus cash can be drawn are most concerned with cash flow and maintaining liquidity (the availability of ready cash). Better-endowed private colleges and universities are less concerned. Public institutions were once untroubled by their cash positions because the "full faith and credit" of the state government backed up their obligations — that is, if the institution couldn't pay, the state would cover the bill. However, as state governments experienced their own economic problems and realized the importance of cash to finance their own operations, some states began delaying payments on the obligations of their public universities and other state agencies. This soured university relations with local vendors, and resulted not only in lost discounts for early or timely payments but also in delays in delivery and even demands for payment in advance.

Two liquidity ratios, most relevant to private institutions, seem particularly useful as possible criteria to assess financial distress, especially at the institutional level. However, in most situations, these ratios would be *secondary and supportive* of other evidence and not sufficient, in and of themselves, to prompt a declaration of exigency.

1. <u>Cash and short-term investments as a percentage of short-term liabilities</u>. "Short-term investments" are assets convertible to cash within the current year, such as bank certificates of deposit, U.S. treasury bills, and commercial paper (loans to private corporations). "Short-term liabilities" are bills or debts that must be paid within the current year. The most reliable measure of liquidity is the *"available funds ratio."* Unlike other measures of liquidity (e.g., "current" and "quick" ratios), the available funds ratio omits receivables (i.e., money owed to the institution on outstanding invoices) and inventories and allows the institution to identify its true cash position. Fiscally responsible colleges and universities seek to keep this available funds ratio at a standard of 0.75, which means that they possess $0.75 in cash and short-term investments for every $1.00 in short-term liabilities. Presumably, a ratio at that level allows bills to be paid on time and minimizes interest owed on short-term debt (e.g., tax anticipation notes for government agencies). A higher education institution might set a lower threshold to signal financial exigency, such as 0.50 or 0.25. It might also focus on unrestricted, short-term assets and liabilities in calculating the ratio.

2. <u>Aging of receivables and payables</u>. Colleges and universities should periodically categorize their "accounts receivable" (what they are owed) and "accounts payable" (what they owe) by the number of days the invoices have remained unpaid: less than 30 days, 30-60 days, more than 60 days, and so on. This categorizing is called "aging." An early warning sign, or criterion, of financial distress is a lengthening in the average age for receivables, followed shortly after that by a similar lengthening in satisfying accounts payable. A standard should also be established that defines an "overdue" account (usually one that is unpaid for more than 30 days). Once *average* agings exceed this 30-day mark, or probably higher, a declaration of financial distress may be considered.

Interfund borrowing and nonmandatory transfers pose the same threat to the reliability of cash flow definitions as criteria for declaring financial distress as they did to budget deficits. Cash can be shifted between the current fund, to which measures of liquidity are applied, and the plant and endowment funds, for example. A disingenuous administration could manipulate its cash position in this way in order to fail the tests for available funds and agings, assert a financial exigency, and fire tenured faculty. Thus, what is needed is an indicator that measures the total resources and obligations of the institution, and not just those of one of its funds or fund groups. (Adoption of the new accounting standard FAS 117 or a "global accounts" approach to financial reporting may achieve this consolidation. These two approaches are examined later in this paper.)

Drops in Student Enrollment

A third measure of operating results is student enrollment. Tuition and fees are the primary sources of revenue for private institutions. These two sources represent, on average, 50 percent of total revenue; although small, modestly endowed private colleges often derive 90 percent or more of their revenue from them (Chabotar and Honan, 1990:29). Increasingly, public institutions are also becoming dependent on such student charges, as state appropriations decline. At research and land-grant universities, student charges as a percentage of total revenue are about 15 percent; state support has dropped below 40 percent (Taylor et al., 1993:4-6). The president of a public institution is alleged to have said that his institution "used to be almost totally state-funded, is now state-supported, and, if the legislature keeps cutting appropriations, will soon only be state-located."

THE PRESIDENT OF A PUBLIC INSTITUTION IS ALLEGED TO HAVE SAID THAT HIS INSTITUTION "USED TO BE ALMOST TOTALLY STATE-FUNDED, IS NOW STATE-SUPPORTED, AND, IF THE LEGISLATURE KEEPS CUTTING APPROPRIATIONS, WILL SOON ONLY BE STATE-LOCATED."

For public and private institutions, funds for research projects and especially student aid have not kept up with the rise in college costs or inflation. Even federal support for work-study and loan programs is threatened. The current pattern of reduced government funding is, according to Robert Rosenzweig (1990:A44), former president of the Association of American Universities, more than a temporary problem:

> There has been a sea change in the views of policy makers in the United States . . .
> about the financing of higher education. It takes different forms in different places, but

the overriding fact is that governments now expect more from their universities but want to pay less for it.

As budgetary dependence on tuition and fees grows, a drop in student enrollment becomes a more significant criterion for financial distress. Both Bennington College and St. Bonaventure University pointed to steep enrollment declines as reasons they had to declare financial emergencies. The chief financial officer at St. Bonaventure argued that its finances

> . . . are highly student-enrollment dependent. Approximately 90 percent of revenue is derived from tuition, fees, housing and food services . . . Without question, a 24 percent decrease in undergraduate enrollment over five years is substantial at any institution. However, at a student-enrollment-dependent institution, it is life threatening (Zekan, 1995:27).

He added that enrollment slides are especially serious when expenses continue to rise and the institution has few liquid investments "with which to weather the downward financial spiral." Bond-rating agencies also consider student demand to be among the *most critical factors* in assessing creditworthiness, especially in schools with high tuition dependence (Forrester, 1988:22,91). Considering market competition, these agencies evaluate admissions and matriculation (yield) rates, student/faculty ratios, and student enrollment on a full-time equivalent (FTE) basis. Measuring student enrollment by simple head count (number of students regardless of courseload) can skew the data. Thus, possible criteria for gauging the significance of enrollment declines include these:

1. <u>Admissions and yield rates for new students</u>. New students include both first-year students and transfers. The higher the number of applicants, the more likely a college or university can admit a low percentage of them and still have a yield (number of students accepting/attending) sufficient to meet its goals. Most institutions aim to admit a low percentage of applicants to prove the institution's selectivity and achieve a high yield rate to evidence their attractiveness. Standards of impending crisis might be a large increase in the admissions/admit rate or a drop in the yield rate — changes in both of 10-20 percent over one to two years, for example. A secondary criterion would be an equivalent change in the *annual retention rate* (Dickmeyer and Hughes, 1980:35), especially between the students' first and second years.

2. <u>Fall FTE enrollment this year as a percentage of fall FTE enrollment last year</u>. If an institution cannot obtain exact FTE numbers because of its mix of full- and part-time students, the numbers can be estimated by adding full-time students and one-third of the part-time students. This fall FTE index or percentage can also be subdivided by class or school.

How far must enrollment drop before financial distress is indicated? In general, the more tuition-dependent and endowment-poor the institution or program, the smaller the enrollment drop required. Any enrollment drop that actually or potentially leads to a budget deficit or cash flow problem of sufficient magnitude for a financial crisis (applying the standards described in previous sections) might qualify. Institutions typically do not have percentage or absolute definitions of troublesome enrollment declines. For example, Colby-Sawyer (1995:34) has defined an "enrollment exigency" as a situation:

> where there is a drop in total full-time enrollment brought about by outside factors such as market shifts, state or federal student aid policy changes, economic hardship in the market area of the institution, or other similar reasons.

Finally, when enrollment declines, institutions should not be expected to invest increasing amounts in financial aid to stabilize it to avoid financial distress. Such a shift argues for an analysis of net tuition per student (tuition and fee revenue less financial aid expenditures), along with enrollment levels, and a standard of how much an institution can discount tuition before the alarm is sounded. Typically, research and land-grant universities use institutional grant aid to discount student tuition about a third. In private institutions, there is a strong but imperfect inverse relationship between tuition and financial aid: The higher the tuition, the lower the percentage of institutional grant aid (Taylor, et al., 1993:88). A private college with low tuition and increasing pressure on grant aid might decide to set a ceiling on grant aid of 40 or 50 percent of tuition and fee revenue. Then enrollment could be allowed to drop by a fixed percentage or absolute amount before the institution was declared to be reaching financial exigency.

Net Worth

To accountants, net worth is the difference between assets (what you own) and liabilities (what you owe). It is a measure of institutional wealth that increases with budget surpluses and decreases with deficits. A commonly accepted indicator of financial stress is negative net worth — i.e., liabilities exceed assets because of chronic budget deficits. Negative net worth is more comprehensive a criterion than is an annual budget deficit because the calculation considers balance sheet resources (assets and liabilities) in the equation. It is also more reliable, since net worth expresses the cumulative effect of deficits and surpluses over more than a single, possibly atypical, year. That is why negative net worth is also known as "accumulated deficits." Except in extremely decentralized colleges or universities (e.g., Harvard) that treat programs and units as virtually autonomous entities, net worth is typically an institution-wide yardstick for financial distress.

Traditional nonprofit fund accounting uses the term "fund balance" rather than "net worth." In such a fund system, each fund has its own set of assets, liabilities, revenues, expenditures, and its own fund balance. That is one problem with using net worth to signal financial distress: Which fund or funds will be examined?

Another problem with net worth as a criterion is that colleges and universities often mix "capital" expenditures (for long-lived assets such as equipment and buildings) with "operating" expenditures (for salaries, benefits, travel, utilities) used for instruction and other activities of the current fiscal year. Some institutions allow capital expenditures that properly belong in the physical plant fund to creep into the current fund by setting a high dollar threshold for charges to plant, or by being inconsistent from year to year. Others carefully segregate capital from operating expenditures but fail to include depreciation expense or another capital consumption charge among their operating expenditures. ("Depreciation" expense is an allowance for "wear and tear" on buildings and other capital assets. It is usually computed by dividing the asset's purchase price by its estimated useful life in years. Thus, a $5 million residence hall with a life expectancy of fifty years would add $100,000 per year to operating expenditures. The fifty-year life expectancy could also have been expressed as "an annual depreciation of 2 percent." A "capital consumption charge" also recognizes such "wear and tear" but is an estimated annual expense not figured solely on the years of useful life.)

> SUCH PRACTICES MAY UNDERESTIMATE THE REAL COSTS OF DELIVERING SERVICES BUT ALLOW THE INSTITUTION TO CLAIM A BALANCED BUDGET.

Such practices may underestimate the real costs of delivering services but allow the institution to claim a balanced budget. In a 1981 study of higher education finance (Jenny, 1981:9), the addition to operating expenditures of even a modest capital consumption charge of 1.5 percent of reported investments in plant assets had drastic results. About 80 percent of the 121 sampled institutions would have incurred operating deficits at the very time that most of them had been reporting balanced operating budgets.

For example, using only operating expenditures, Bowdoin College calculated that the cost per student in FY 1994-95 exceeded $40,000. But the cost rose to more than $43,000 if the College included depreciation. (This assumes a $250 million plant with 2 percent depreciation spread over fifteen hundred students.) The addition of depreciation would also have transformed a reported budget surplus of $200,000 into a $5 million deficit.

Finally, traditional accounting practice commonly values assets not at their market value (what they might sell for) or replacement cost but at their original, historical cost ("book value"). This seriously distorts any assessment of the institution's current net worth, affecting that criterion's legitimacy as a basis for asserting financial distress. For years, for example, Harvard University refused to include a plant fund in its financial statements for this distortion reason. Founded in 1636, and with buildings one hundred years old or more, the university felt that valuing its physical plant at original cost would produce, as one official said, "a nonsense number." This potential for distortion argues for the use of current market values, even estimated ones.

Assuming, then, that assets are valued at market, possible criteria for the assessment of net worth include these:

1. <u>Expendable fund balances as a percentage of total expenditures and mandatory transfers</u>. This ratio examines the institution's capacity to sustain normal operations without considering revenues from operations (such as tuition or state appropriations). "Expendable" fund balances in the numerator are measured at year-end and include current funds, quasi-endowment funds, and plant funds: both restricted and unrestricted. The denominator is drawn from the current fund alone. KPMG Peat Marwick (1987:15) recommends a standard 0.3:1 ratio — i.e., at least $0.30 in expendable fund balances for every $1.00 of expenditures and transfers. Smaller proportions of expendable fund balances signal a weak financial condition. Declining percentages mean that expendable fund balances are not increasing at the same rate as are expenditures, thus eroding institutional flexibility.

2. <u>Unrestricted current fund assets less unrestricted current fund liabilities</u>. Since most budgets are based in the current fund, this ratio is a fundamental indicator of financial health. Chronic budget deficits erode current fund assets and the fund balance to the point where liabilities exceed assets. "Negative net worth" is a bankruptcy gauge for corporations. For colleges and universities, the standard for financial exigency here might be: (1) as soon as the current fund balance goes negative, or (2) when the negative fund balance reaches an absolute dollar figure or percentage of assets, e.g., 20 percent.

Bond Ratings

A composite approach to the definition of financial distress at the institutional level is offered by bond ratings. A "rating" is a measure of the likelihood of timely and complete repayment of principal and interest on the debt incurred by issuing a bond.

Independent rating agencies analyze and rate the creditworthiness of public and private colleges and other institutions that are seeking to issue bonds, typically to obtain funds for new buildings and major renovations. Most institutions cannot afford to pay millions of dollars for construction projects out of their operating budgets, and cannot count on large capital gifts and grants. More important, interest received by investors on such bonds is usually exempt from federal, and sometimes state and local, income taxes. For this reason, investors are willing to accept lower rates of interest than they would earn on corporate bonds or other taxable investments, resulting in lower borrowing costs for the college or university. Even institutions with substantial quasi-endowments borrow money at low tax exempt rates for certain projects rather than use endowment funds and lose their potentially higher rates of return.

The two major rating agencies are Standard and Poor's (S&P) and Moody's Investors. The better the institution's creditworthiness, the higher its rating. And, most important, the higher its rating, the lower the interest rate the institution must offer to attract investors.

Bond ratings fall into two categories: investment grade and noninvestment grade. For example, Moody's investment-grade ratings range from *Aaa* to *Baa*. *Aaa* bonds have the highest rating because they have been judged to carry the least risk that bondholders will not be repaid. *Aa* are very strong, with slightly more investment risk. *A* bonds are strong, with good security for principal and interest payments, but factors are present that could impair repayment in the future (e.g., declining applications for admission). The minimum investment-grade rating of *Baa* means that interest payments and principal security appear adequate now but could be unreliable over the long term. (The equivalent to Moody's *Baa* in Standard & Poor's rating system is *BBB*.)

Noninvestment-grade bonds (*Ba* and lower in Moody's, *BBB-* and lower in S&P's) have high interest costs because their speculative nature and the higher risk of default mean institutions must offer higher rates to attract investors. Many endowments and pension funds are forbidden by their charters to invest in such bonds. Fortunately, comparatively few colleges or universities have been rated this low. In 1993, S&P gave noninvestment-grade bond ratings to no public universities and fewer than 5 percent of private colleges (King, et al., 1994:142-143). In 1996, Moody's gave noninvestment-grade ratings to only two private colleges, including Bennington, and no public colleges or universities (Moody's, 1996:1,13).

When issuing a bond rating for a college or university, the agencies consider many criteria

FIGURE 1
IMPORTANT BOND RATING CRITERIA

	DESIRABLE TRENDS/LEVELS
STUDENT DEMAND	
• Enrollment	stable or increasing
• Selectivity (Admit) Rate *% of applicants offered admission*	lower
• Matriculation (Yield) Rate *% of admitted students who accept/attend*	higher
• Student:Faculty Ratio	lower
FINANCIAL CONDITION	
• Tuition Dependency *tuition as a % of total revenue, excluding auxiliaries*	lower
• Tuition Discount *grant aid as a % of tuition and fees*	lower
• Fund Balance as a % of Total Expenses *unrestricted current fund only*	higher
• Total Endowment	higher
• % Quasi-Endowment	higher
• Endowment per FTE Student *including quasi-endowment*	higher
• Debt	lower
• Debt Service as a % of Total Expenses	lower
• Endowment as a % of Total Debt *endowment at market value*	higher

discussed earlier, including budget surpluses and deficits, endowment, and enrollment. The *better* the institution's performance, the higher the bond rating. Important criteria are listed in **Figure 1**, along with the desired trend or level of any standards (Forrester, 1988:22,91-94; Standard & Poor's, 1991).

In 1995, based on bond ratings of 116 private institutions and 97 public institutions, Moody's (1995b:8) found that several of these criteria correlated most strongly with the rating level. For private institutions receiving a noninvestment-grade rating (*Ba/BBB –* and lower), the median values on these criteria were: selectivity (80.1%); matriculation (51.5%); tuition dependency (70.1%); tuition discount (41.5%); endowment per student ($5,151); and endowment to debt (89.9%). There were too few cases for public institutions to provide similar medians.

> WHILE THE CRITERIA THAT THE RATING AGENCIES CONSIDER ARE RELATIVELY STABLE, THE STANDARDS THE INSTITUTIONS MUST MEET TO RECEIVE PARTICULAR RATINGS CHANGE FROM YEAR TO YEAR, DEPENDING ON INDUSTRY TRENDS AND ECONOMIC CONDITIONS.

While the criteria that the rating agencies consider are relatively stable, the standards the institutions must meet to receive particular ratings change from year to year, depending on industry trends and economic conditions. For example, Moody's 1996 (1) medians for noninvestment-grade ratings were considerably different from 1995's, especially in selectivity (68.9% versus 80.1% in 1995), matriculation (29.5% versus 51.5%), and endowment to debt (148.6% versus 89.9%). No one criterion governs, and a college or university does not have to meet the standard on every criterion to achieve a particular rating.

These rating factors suggest two possible criteria of financial exigency sufficient to justify the layoff of tenured faculty:

1.	<u>Downgrade in bond rating to a noninvestment grade</u> (i.e., *Ba/BBB –* and lower). However, an institution can avoid receiving a noninvestment-grade rating — and even achieve a *Aaa* rating — by purchasing insurance that ensures repayment or by pledging its endowment and other assets as collateral. Also, many states issue and guarantee bonds on behalf of mixed groups of colleges, hospitals, and other nonprofits; the rating is based on the state's creditworthiness, not on the financial condition of any one of its institutions. Thus, any standard for financial exigency would have to ask: *What would the institution's bond rating have been without insurance, collateral, or state guarantees?*

2.	<u>Violation of bond covenants</u>. These covenants contain criteria and standards, similar to those analyzed for a bond rating, that the institution promises to meet every year during the term of the bonds. The institution must file an annual report that relies on audited financial statements and other data to certify whether it has met the terms of the covenant (e.g., enrollment, debt service percentages, endowment). If the institution violates the covenants, public authorities or trustees acting on behalf of the bondholders may declare the bonds in default or apply increased interest charges. Sometimes there is a grace period during which the institution can correct the problem or take another action specified in the covenant (e.g., hire a retrenchment consultant) to avoid penalties.

The advantages of these two criteria to signal financial exigency are that they are well known and reasonably quantitative. They are also multivariate by considering a range of financial and student indicators. They speak to institutional survival, as does the AAUP's definition, but may be provoked before fiscal collapse. Their objectivity is protected by having the ratings issued by independent experts. Finally, the qualitative judgment of the experts in the rating agency counts almost as much as the quantitative data — which also can be viewed as a limitation.

On the other hand, the limitations of bond ratings criteria are significant. Very few institutions are ever downgraded to noninvestment grade; witness the presence of just two private colleges in the 1996 Moody's survey. Most financially troubled institutions might ask for a "preliminary review" by the rating agency prior to issuing new bonds but withdraw if the rating is likely to be below the minimum investment grade of *Baa* or *BBB*. If the poor preliminary rating were made known at the institution — an unlikely event — that might be viewed as tantamount to a downgrade and result in a declaration of financial exigency.

THE ADVANTAGES OF THESE TWO CRITERIA TO SIGNAL FINANCIAL EXIGENCY ARE THAT THEY ARE WELL KNOWN AND REASONABLY QUANTITATIVE.

A slightly less drastic measure might be to include a downgrade to the minimum investment grade of *Baa* or *BBB* in addition to the noninvestment grades below *Baa* or *BBB* in defining financial exigency. In 1996, about forty private institutions examined by Moody's were rated *Baa* or below, or about 25 percent of the total. That same year, only seven public colleges and universities, 6 percent, were rated that low.

Also, a bond rating takes a long-term perspective on the institution's capacity to repay principal and interest. A college might have a low bond rating not because it is in *imminent* financial danger — a legitimate trigger of faculty layoffs — but because it is judged unlikely to meet its debt payment *five or ten years* in the future. This implies that financial exigency should depend on (1) a downgrade of an existing rating to the minimum investment grade of *Baa* or *BBB* or any of the noninvestment grades below and (2) substantial current budget deficits without offsetting endowment or other resources.

Finally, some observers of the rating agencies claim that the number and qualifications of the analysts assigned to nonprofit bond issues are inferior to those committed to the agencies' corporate clients. And since the financial data needed for the ratings typically are based in traditional fund accounting practices, the data are affected by the same problems that such accounting poses for budget deficits and similar criteria for financial exigency.

Alternatives to Traditional Accounting

In recent years, debate has escalated about the merits of traditional accounting for accurate and understandable financial analysis and reporting. The practices of segregating resources into separate funds, interfund transfers and borrowing, valuing assets at historical cost, and neglecting capital costs have contributed to a lack of confidence in using traditional accounting methods to define yardsticks for financial distress. "The administration must be hiding something" is the typical response when faculty or student leaders confront a college or university financial statement.

Two alternatives now exist to traditional fund accounting. The first is optional, and arises from the research of Gordon Winston on *global accounts*. The second is required, at least for private institutions, by *new accounting standards* issued in 1993 by the Financial Accounting Standards Board.

Global Accounts

Developed by Gordon Winston, of Williams College, global accounts are based on the premises that fund accounts are hard to understand, and focus on only part of a college's economic activity, i.e., on its operating budget and endowment. The traditional valuation of assets at historical cost is also deceptive. For a college in financial distress (and, presumably, considering the elimination of tenured faculty), Winston (1993:20) argues that the obscurity created by traditional fund accounting

> . . . is too easily seen as obfuscation — evidence of hanky-panky by the administration or board that's intended to wring unnecessary concessions from one group on campus or another, or from taxpayers.

In contrast, global accounts attempt to answer three questions: (1) How much did the college take in during the year — from all sources ("*global income*")? (2) What did it do with that money ("*global expenditures*")? and (3) What effect did all that have on the college's real *total wealth*?

Besides examining a college's financial wealth (revenues, expenditures, and endowment), global accounts include its physical wealth, because the consuming of physical wealth should be counted as the institution's current costs of doing business. To this end, global accounts report the value of physical plant, equipment, and land in current replacement terms as the basis for measuring actual depreciation. They also report the "opportunity cost" during the year of investing the institution's wealth in such physical assets instead of in the endowment and other alternatives. (For example, if a $5 million building is presumed to have a market value that appreciates 4 percent per year at a time when the annual total return on the endowment is 10 percent, the opportunity cost of that choice — of building over endowment — is roughly 6 percent, or $300,000 per year. Since many academic buildings have little or no resale value, the opportunity costs would likely be higher.)

So both depreciation and opportunity cost are recognized as costs of operation. The "bottom line" in global accounts is *saving,* calculated as global income less global current expenditures, where expenditures include all such capital costs. When an institution's income is greater than its expenditures, it has positive saving and adds to its total wealth. Saving can be used to add to financial investments or to add new property or buildings. When income is less than expenditures, the institution draws on net wealth from the past.

According to Winston, the use of global accounts added $77 million to Harvard's reported operating costs in FY 1990-91 and prompted a reported deficit of $42 million. On the positive side, measurement of physical capital wealth with the global accounts approach often significantly increases reported institutional wealth. Thus, Harvard's endowment of $7.8 billion at the end of FY 1994-95 would be only part of its total wealth of about $11 billion.

In time-series analysis, global accounts also adjust for inflation. Bowdoin College's endowment of $270 million would have to grow to $280 million just to preserve its purchasing power in a year of 4 percent inflation, for example. In an analysis of Williams College, average *real* saving adjusted for inflation over a five-year period was 40 percent less than nominal saving without an inflation adjustment (Weber and Winston, 1994:8).

Where does this leave the definition of financial exigency? Using global accounts, standards and criteria can be written in terms of real saving, total wealth, or both:

1.   <u>Annual saving this year is "negative" and "too large."</u> This criterion examines the inflation-adjusted, real saving and would be triggered by dis-saving that was unacceptably large. "Too large" could be judged as a percentage of income or a percentage of total wealth. For example, a college might include among its yardsticks for financial distress a drop in real saving (revenue was less than expenditures) equivalent to 10 percent of income. Again, to damp the effects of transient fluctuations,

these figures should be smoothed over several years.

2. <u>Total wealth this year as a percentage of total wealth last year</u>. This is a measure of real saving over time. Perhaps a "large" decline in real wealth for three or more years would be considered severe enough to declare exigency and lay off tenured faculty. For example, its $1 billion in deferred maintenance might have qualified Yale for financial exigency using a global accounts approach, since the inclusion of depreciation in its global accounts would have signaled a financial crisis far earlier than would have traditional accounting practices (Winston, 1994:13).

New Accounting Standards

Most private colleges and universities adopted new accounting standards in FY 1995-96 that transform fund accounting and their financial reporting. These are Financial Accounting Standards (FAS) 116, *Accounting for Contributions Received and Contributions Made*, and FAS 117, *Financial Statements of Not-for-Profit Organizations* (Financial Accounting Standards Board, 1993a and b).

THE INTENT WITH THE NEW STANDARD IS TO MAKE NONPROFIT FINANCIAL REPORTS MORE LIKE CORPORATE STATEMENTS, AS WELL AS EASIER TO READ AND ANALYZE.

FAS 116 modifies accounting standards for contributions and applies to organizations that make contributions and also to those that receive contributions. Under the new provisions, private colleges and universities must record unconditional promises to give, or pledges, as revenues in the period the pledge was received, even if the cash or noncash contribution has not yet been collected. In addition, the amount of the pledge must be recognized as an asset on the institution's balance sheet as "pledges receivable." Both the revenue and the asset should be reduced by allowances for uncollectible amounts and discounts for pledges receivable over more than one year.

FAS 117 is much like global accounting, differing largely in its treatment of physical capital costs. FAS 117 alters financial reporting by changing its focus from fund groups to the entity as a whole, based on the existence or absence of donor-imposed restrictions. Funds will still exist; they just will not be separately reported on audited financial statements. Instead of the many funds formerly used, colleges and universities must classify their revenues and expenses (and assets and liabilities) into one of three categories: unrestricted, temporarily restricted, and restricted. Assets minus liabilities is now "net assets" instead of "fund balance." The intent with the new standard is to make nonprofit financial reports more like corporate statements, as well as easier to read and analyze. It was also designed to remove reporting inconsistencies among nonprofits (e.g., hospitals, colleges, and voluntary organizations) and reduce confusion over just what reporting principles were generally accepted (Financial Accounting Standards Board, 1994:2/1-14).

By not allowing the distributing of expenses across several funds, and discouraging interfund transactions, FAS 117 in particular may provide a superior measure of operating results for the college or university. This is especially true since depreciation on funds invested in physical assets will now be recognized as an operating expense, which is an objective of the global accounts approach discussed earlier. Thus, FAS 117 has the potential of increasing the reliability of budget deficits, cash flow, and net worth as criteria for financial exigency.

On the other hand, "colleges and universities are likely to appear wealthier after adopting FAS 116 and 117" (Moody's, 1995a:2). In fact, these new standards may exaggerate the financial strength of many institutions. Revenues and assets may appear much higher than previously reported, though the amounts available for operations — and to remedy financial distress — may be small.

Why is that? By recognizing pledges as revenues, FAS 116 may result in budget surpluses ballooning and, because this standard reports pledges receivable as an asset, net worth will also rise. Further, many gifts formerly accounted for as endowments and other capital additions (used for construction and renovation) will be recognized under FAS 117 as unrestricted income, also increasing budget surpluses and net worth. For example, Bowdoin College has a balanced budget in its unrestricted fund in FY 1994-95 using traditional fund accounting but a $16 million estimated surplus (or "change in net assets") using the new FAS standards. Even private colleges with large operating budget deficits or eroding cash flow may have difficulty proving to themselves or others that financial exigency exists when they are well endowed or in the midst of a capital campaign.

FAS 116 and 117 are not expected to have an impact on bond ratings, since "these new accounting standards do not alter the economic realities of colleges and universities" (Moody's, 1995a:2). However, the rating agencies are expected to request supplementary information from colleges and universities that may not be disclosed in audited financial statements under the new standards. Furthermore, the agencies have developed new financial ratios using FAS 116 and 117 that

> REVENUES AND ASSETS MAY APPEAR MUCH HIGHER THAN PREVIOUSLY REPORTED, THOUGH THE AMOUNTS AVAILABLE FOR OPERATIONS — AND TO REMEDY FINANCIAL DISTRESS — MAY BE SMALL.

are likely to correlate highly with credit ratings assigned to private colleges and universities. Moody's, for example, believes that it needed the new ratios because "financial measures and medians cannot be readily converted to the new formats required by FAS 116 and 117" (1995a:2).

Using the new FAS standards, five possible ratios seem especially suited to deciding whether a financial crisis is at hand (Moody's, 1995a:8-13; KPMG Peat Marwick, 1995:5-23):

1.   <u>Expendable resources as a percentage of long-term debt</u>. "Expendable resources" denotes the total institutional net assets, unrestricted and temporarily restricted, available for expenditure. Ratios significantly below 100 percent might suggest financial exigency. KPMG Peat Marwick (1995:6) holds that this ratio is a "viability ratio" and "one of the most basic determinants of financial health."

2.   <u>Change in net assets as a percentage of total net assets</u>. This ratio considers the annual change in total net assets. Since most colleges and universities carry their physical plant at historical cost, a revaluation to replacement cost or current market value is necessary for a realistic result. Finally, because net assets fluctuates due to the recognition of pledges and endowment market value, the ratio should be considered only over three to five years, which smooths out the data. To declare financial exigency, the standard might well be a real decline in net assets over such a time period, after discounting for inflation.

3.   <u>Change in unrestricted net assets as a percentage of total unrestricted income</u>. This ratio comes closest to measuring the conventional budget surplus or deficit. A negative percentage sustained over two or more years might signal financial distress.

4.   <u>Unrestricted and temporarily restricted net assets (excluding plant) as a percentage of short-term debt</u>. Since poor cash flow and insufficient liquidity are often associated with financial exigency, this ratio may be especially useful. A ratio below 200 percent is troubling, and below 100 percent may be disastrous.

5.   <u>Total resources ($) per FTE student</u>. This ratio compares the total net assets, except amounts invested in plant facilities, to the full-time equivalent number of students. The smaller the ratio, the less capacity the institution has to invest in the academic program or to cope with emergencies.

Institutions adopting financial yardsticks to measure financial distress under FAS 116-117 should consider separating their operating from nonoperating transactions:

•   Operating revenues (e.g., tuition and fees, government aid, auxiliary services, and endowment earnings used) would be available to finance activities and operating expenses (e.g., instruction and student services) of the current period. Any endowment earnings used (income and capital gains) must be considered a "reasonable amount" under a board-approved spending formula, typically 4-6 percent of market value.

- Nonoperating revenues are not normally available for the current period, and include new endowment gifts, unrealized gains on investments, and investments in plant. (Whatever the institution does, bond-rating agencies usually exclude institutional equity invested in plant facilities in analyzing college and university finances.)

An institution should set separate standards for financial exigency based on *operating* versus *total* revenues and expenses. For example, a college might decide that financial distress would be asserted in the event of an unrestricted operating deficit (decrease in net assets) of 10 percent over two years and/or a total deficit of 5 percent over the same period.

The Financial Accounting Standards Board requires FAS 116-117 be adopted by most private colleges and universities by FY 1995-96; small private institutions (less than $5 million in total assets and $1 million total expenses) have until FY 1996-97. Neither standard applies to public colleges and universities, since they follow regulations published not by the FASB but by the Governmental Accounting Standards Board (GASB). GASB, too, is considering similar changes to its reporting standards (Moody's: 1995a:1).

INSTITUTIONAL CHOICE

For trustees and other policymakers in search of an appropriate definition of financial exigency, **Figure 2** on the next page summarizes the significant advantages and limitations of the yardsticks discussed in this paper.

Current Practice

In sum, the most prevalent yardsticks for declaring financial exigency for the purpose of terminating tenured faculty appear to be budget deficits accompanied by declining enrollment. These criteria are relevant both institution-wide and at the program or unit level. In private institutions, a real decline in the market value of the endowment because of its overuse to support the operating

FIGURE 2
ADVANTAGES AND LIMITATIONS OF ALTERNATIVE YARDSTICKS

	ADVANTAGES	LIMITATIONS
OPERATING RESULTS		
• BUDGET DEFICITS	Relevant to both institution-wide and program/unit distress	Overlooks other available assets*
	Broadly understood and widely used	Can be manipulated*
• CASH FLOW PROBLEMS	Relevant to institution as a whole	Can be manipulated*
	Indicator of short-term operating problems	Secondary measure
• DROPS IN ENROLLMENT	Relevant to both institution-wide and program/unit distress	Definition of "large" drop
	Critical for institutions w/high tuition dependence	Less critical for public institutions w/low tuition dependence
	Broadly understood and widely used	
	Very significant for bond-rating agencies	
NET WORTH	Relevant to institution as a whole	Assets often valued at historical cost*
	Considers not only revenue and expense but also assets and liabilities	Mixes operating and capital costs*
	Cumulative indicator -- not based on one year	Choice of fund(s)*
BOND RATINGS	Relevant to institution as a whole	Few institutions are ever downgraded significantly
	Broadly understood	Ratings take long-term perspective v. short-term crisis
	Consider quantitative and qualitative criteria	
	Objective	

* May be improved by implementation of FAS 116 and 117

budget also seems a convincing but supporting rationale. In concert with global accounts and new accounting standards, these measures have heightened reliability. Bond ratings, expressed either in terms of a downgrade to the minimum investment grade or below or a reassessment upon violation of bond covenants, hold significant promise as criteria if the ratings are confirmed by budget deficits and other short-term warning indicators.

Whatever yardsticks are adopted should be published, if not in a faculty handbook, then at least in some administrative or board policy manual. It is also not essential to hold fast to "exigency" as the term of choice. Institutions could well use other labels such as "crisis" or "emergency." Better still, they could avoid any one label and simply define the financial conditions that warrant the layoff of tenured faculty.

Samples

The challenge for individual colleges and universities will be to adopt measures and yardsticks of financial distress that reflect the institution's particular circumstances. We have argued throughout this paper that *effective* statements of financial exigency are clear and specific — conditions met by few institutions. It is the failure to define precisely what is meant by "financial exigency" that confuses the issue and compounds the problem. For example, Fairleigh Dickinson, which adopted the AAUP interpretation, states in its faculty contract:

> The University shall not declare a state of financial exigency unless it is demonstrably <u>bona fide</u>. Financial exigency shall be defined as an emergency condition in which the University's continued existence is in serious jeopardy for financial reasons (Rhoades, 1993:323).

What would a "clear and specific" statement look like? Such a statement that attempts to incorporate suitable yardsticks might stipulate:

> Financial exigency at XYZ University shall be defined as the existence of two or more of the following conditions: (1) a downgrade of the institution's bond rating to the minimum investment grade of *Baa* or *BBB* or below in a given year; (2) an operating budget deficit equivalent to 3 percent or more and that is greater than last year's; (3) three or more years of decline in FTE enrollment; and (4) real decline in the market value of the endowment, adjusted for inflation, for three or more years.

> A localized financial exigency at XYZ Program might be defined as some combination of (2)

and (3). A concern that layoffs of tenured faculty must be the last resort in this situation might be addressed by adding after "conditions" the phrase "which could not be adequately alleviated by means other than the dismissal of tenured faculty." Again, our purpose here is not to recommend a particular statement, but rather to suggest appropriate language, protecting both the institution and the faculty, that such a statement might contain.

* * *

This paper has attempted to offer and illustrate a wide range of measures of financial distress, — ranging from familiar budget deficits and enrollment drops to innovative indices based on "global accounts" and new accounting standards. That financial distress and faculty tenure have been connected here reflects reality and not necessarily our agenda or that of the sponsors of this paper. That tenure is threatened by the lack of specific and understandable criteria for financially based layoffs of tenured faculty also reflects reality. It has been our goal to suggest alternative ways that colleges and universities can resolve their dilemma decisively, fairly, and, especially, credibly. ■

REFERENCES

American Association of University Professors. *Recommended Institutional Regulations on Academic Freedom and Tenure.* Washington, DC: 1982.

Arenson, Karen W. "CUNY Board Decides Crisis Over Aid Cuts," *The New York Times* (March 26, 1996), pp. B1, B5.

Chabotar, Kent John. "Financial Ratio Analysis Comes to Nonprofits," *The Journal of Higher Education* (March/April, 1989), pp. 188-208.

——————— . "Managing Participative Budgeting in Higher Education," *Change* (September/October, 1995), pp. 21-29.

———————, and James P. Honan. "Coping With Retrenchment: Strategies and Tactics," *Change* (November/December, 1990), pp. 28-34.

Colby-Sawyer College. *Faculty Handbook.* New London, NH: 1995.

Dembner, Alice. "Bennington Sets Bold Restructuring: Tuition, Faculty Cuts Signal New Realities," *The Boston Globe* (June 26, 1994), p. 21.

Dickmeyer, Nathan, and K. Scott Hughes. *Financial Self-Assessment: A Workbook for Colleges*. Washington, DC: National Association of College and University Business Officers, 1980.

Douglas, J.M. *Directory of Faculty Contracts and Bargaining Agents in Institutions of Higher Education*. New York: National Center for the Study of Collective Bargaining in Higher Education and the Professions, CUNY, 1990.

Financial Accounting Standards Board. *Statement of Financial Accounting Standards No. 116: Accounting for Contributions Received and Contributions Made*. Norwalk, CT: FASB, 1993a.

——————— . *Statement of Financial Accounting Standards No. 117: Financial Statements of Not-for-Profit Organizations*. Norwalk, CT: FASB, 1993b.

——————— . *Accounting and Reporting by Not-for-Profit Organizations: A Comprehensive View of Statements 116 and 117*. Norwalk, CT: FASB, 1994.

Forrester, Robert T. *A Handbook on Debt Management for Colleges and Universities*. Washington, DC: National Association of College and University Business Officers, 1988.

Houpt, Corinne A. "The Age of Austerity: Downsizing for the 90s." In Corinne A. Houpt (ed.), *Academic Program Closures: A Legal Compendium*. Washington, DC: National Association of College and University Attorneys, 1991.

Indiana University Purdue University Indianapolis. *IUPUI Academic Handbook Supplement*. Indianapolis: IUPUI, 1995.

Jenny, Hans J. *Hang-Gliding or Looking for an Updraft: A Study of College and University Finance in the 1980s — The Capital Margin*. Wooster, OH: The College of Wooster, and Boulder, CO: John Minter Associates, 1981.

King, George A., et al. *NACUBO Guide to Issuing and Managing Debt*. Washington, DC: National Association of College and University Business Officers, 1994.

KPMG Peat Marwick. *Ratio Analysis in Higher Education*, 2nd edition. New York, 1987.

——————— . *Ratio Analysis in Higher Education*, 3rd edition. New York, 1995.

Kreiser, B. Robert. "Position of Financial Exigency," *Academe* (May-June, 1985), pp. 61-62.

Lyons, Sheridan. "Essex Community College Ordered to Reinstate Two Tenured Professors," *The Baltimore Sun* (August 11, 1995), p. 3B.

Moody's Investors Services. *Higher Education 1996 Medians, draft.* New York: Moody's, 1996.

——————— . *Moody's Introduces New Financial Ratios for Colleges and Universities.* New York: Moody's, 1995a.

——————— . *Higher Education 1995 Medians.* New York: Moody's, 1995b.

National Association of College and University Business Officers. *Practical Approaches to Rightsizing.* Washington, DC: NACUBO, 1992.

National Center for Education Statistics. *Digest of Educational Statistics, 1993.* Washington, DC: U.S. Department of Education, 1993.

Rhoades, Gary. "Retrenchment Clauses in Faculty Union Contracts," *The Journal of Higher Education* (May/June, 1993), pp. 312-347.

Richards, M.S. " 'Financial Emergency' and the Faculty Furlough: A Breach of Contract?" *Journal of College and University Law* 64 (1991), pp. 65-77.

Rosenzweig, Robert M. "Challenges to Test the Mettle of Academe's Best Leaders," *The Chronicle of Higher Education* (February 28, 1990), p. A44.

Saunders, Marybeth K. "Developing a Financial Exigency Policy for Terminating Personnel," *Educational Record* (Summer, 1984), pp. 42-44.

Standard & Poor's. *Private Colleges and Universities.* New York: S&P, 1991.

Taylor, Barbara, et al. *Strategic Indicators for Higher Education.* Princeton: Peterson's Guides, 1993.

University of Wyoming. *University Regulation 41, Revision 1: Financial Exigency.* Laramie: University of Wyoming, 1993.

Waggaman, John S. *Strategies and Consequences: Managing the Costs in Higher Education.* ASHE-ERIC Higher Education Report No. 8. Washington, DC: The George Washington University, 1991.

Weber, Valerie, and Gordon C. Winston. *The Economic Performance of Williams, Amherst, Swarthmore, and Wellesley 1988-9 to 1992-3: A Global Comparison.* Williamstown: Williams Project on the Economics of Higher Education, 1994.

Weeks, Kent M. "When Financial Exigency Justifies Dismissal," *AGB Reports* (November/December, 1980), pp. 35-40.

Winston, Gordon C. "New Dangers in Old Traditions: The Reporting of Economic Performance in Colleges and Universities," *Change* (January/February, 1993), pp. 18-23.

——————— . "Fiduciary Responsibility and the Depreciation of Fund Accounting," *Trusteeship* (September/October, 1994), pp. 9-14.

——————— . Letter to authors, December 16, 1995.

Zekan, Donald L. "Beyond Financial Exigency: St. Bonaventure's Fiscal Crisis Reflects Economic Realities," *Business Officer* (December, 1995), pp. 24-32.

Zemsky, Robert, and William E. Massy. "Cost Containment: Committing to a New Economic Reality," *Change* (November/December, 1990), pp. 16-22.

<u>PRICES</u>

AAHE Members $8.50 ea
Nonmembers $10.00 ea
(Plus shipping)

<u>ORDER ONLINE</u>
www.aahe.org

<u>NEED MORE INFORMATION?</u>
American Association for Higher Education
One Dupont Circle, Suite 360, Washington, DC 20036-1110
202/293-6440, fax 202/293-0073, pubs@aahe.org

<u>REPRINT PERMISSION</u>
AAHE's New Pathways Project has as one of its missions to disseminate information
and foster discussion. With that purpose in mind, AAHE grants to the purchaser
of this Working Paper permission to photocopy and distribute it for any educational, nonprofit
purpose.

About the New Pathways Series

<u>AAHE ITEM #</u>

#1: MAKING A PLACE FOR THE NEW AMERICAN SCHOLAR   #FR01WP

Presents a richly textured vision of the role of the scholar in a rapidly changing, democratic America. Frames key questions to be addressed in rethinking and restructuring faculty careers. By R. Eugene Rice, scholar-in-residence and director, Forum on Faculty Roles & Rewards, AAHE. (48pp, March 1996)

#2: TENURE SNAPSHOT   #FR02WP

Outlines current areas of concern, ongoing initiatives, and national trends related to academic tenure. Based on a November 1995 AAHE survey distributed to 1,200 four-year college and university provosts, with the intention of building an archive of information on current tenure policies, practices, and trends. By Cathy A. Trower, senior researcher, Harvard University, Graduate School of Education. (32pp, March 1996)

#3: WHERE TENURE DOES NOT REIGN: COLLEGES WITH CONTRACT SYSTEMS   #FR03WP

Presents the experiences of campuses without tenure and campuses where faculty may choose tenure or contracts. Issues covered include academic freedom, faculty recruitment, selectivity, turnover, and reward structures. Answers the question, "What lessons can be learned from campuses with contract systems?" By Richard Chait, professor, and Cathy A. Trower, senior researcher, Harvard University, Graduate School of Education. (34pp, March 1997)

#4: NEW YARDSTICKS TO MEASURE FINANCIAL DISTRESS   **#FRO4WP**

Offers suggestions for new criteria and yardsticks to gauge a college's financial condition, and identifies means to equitably balance employment security for faculty with programmatic flexibility for institutions. By Kent John Chabotar, vice president, business and finance, Bowdoin College; and James P. Honan, lecturer, Harvard University, Graduate School of Education. (38pp, August 1996)

#5: ACADEMIC FREEDOM WITHOUT TENURE?   **#FRO5WP**

Conceptualizes one or more procedures where academic freedom could be uncoupled from academic tenure -- where some other means are offered to ensure the professoriate the unfettered opportunity to teach and conduct research — and explores the tradeoffs involved in doing so. By J. Peter Byrne, professor, Georgetown University Law Center. (25pp, January 1997)

#6: TWO FACULTIES OR ONE? THE CONUNDRUM OF PART-TIMERS IN A BIFURCATED WORKFORCE   **#FRO6WP**

Describes the dual labor market in academe, based on the authors? book The Invisible Faculty, data from the 1993 NCES Survey, and other sources. Focuses on the effect of the dual labor market on tenured and tenure-track faculty, part-time and temporary faculty, and institutions. Explores possible changes that would transform the dual labor market into a more flexible and integrated employment system. By Judith M. Gappa, vice president for human relations, Purdue University; and David W. Leslie, professor of education, College of William and Mary. (36pp, May 1997)

#7: HEEDING NEW VOICES: ACADEMIC CAREERS FOR A NEW GENERATION   **#FRO7WP**

Reports on structured interviews conducted with new faculty and graduate students who will be the professoriate of the future. Considers what changes need to be made in the faculty career to make it more enticing, self-renewing, and resilient for the individual and to provide greater flexibility for institutions. (Includes a "Principles of Good Practice: Supporting Early-Career Faculty" section, which is also available separately.) By R. Eugene Rice, scholar-in-residence and director, AAHE's Forum on Faculty Roles & Rewards; Mary Deane Sorcinelli, associate provost and director, Center for Teaching, University of Massachusetts-Amherst; and Ann E. Austin, associate professor of educational administration, Michigan State University. (60pp, September 2000)

#8: WORK, FAMILY, AND THE FACULTY CAREER   **#FRO8WP**

Examines the conflicts faculty face as they try to balance personal and professional lives throughout their careers; considers actions universities and colleges can take to help. Includes an overview of institutional leadership initiatives, policies, strategies, programs, and practices aimed at reducing the stress these conflicts cause and enhancing the performance and satisfaction of faculty. By Judith M. Gappa, vice president for human relations, Purdue University, and Shelley M. MacDermid, associate professor and director, Center for Families, Purdue University. (40pp, August 1997)

#9: IDEAS IN INCUBATION: THREE POSSIBLE MODIFICATIONS TO TRADITIONAL TENURE POLICIES   **#FRO9WP**

Examines tenure by objectives (a reconfiguration of the probationary period), post-tenure reviews that focus more on departments than on individual faculty performance, and modification of academic freedom without tenure (including a draft policy by Martin Michaelson for discussion). By Richard Chait, professor, Harvard University, Graduate School of Education. (44pp, August 1998)

#10: Off the Tenure Track: Six Models for Full-Time, Nontenurable Appointments #FR10WP

Explores nontraditional, full-time faculty appointments that are being used as alternatives to traditional tenure-track faculty careers, and the academic and other reasons underlying their increasing use. By Judith M. Gappa, vice president for human relations, Purdue University. (44pp, December 1996)

#11: Senior Faculty Considering Retirement: A Developmental & Policy Issue #FR11WP

Examines what influences senior faculty in making decisions about the timing of retirement. Focuses on the interaction between individual development and planning and institutional policies and planning. By Ann Ferren, vice president for academic affairs and professor of education, Radford University. (38pp, March 1998)

#12: Post-Tenure Review: Policies, Practices, Precautions #FR12WP

Reviews current institutional policies and practices aimed at periodically evaluating tenured faculty. Topics examined include: campus goals for post-tenure review; specific evaluation criteria/procedures; implementation considerations and resource implications. Discusses the opportunities and difficulties associated with the initiation of such reviews, and how institutions handle measurement of outcomes and effectiveness. By Christine M. Licata, associate dean for academic affairs, Rochester Institute of Technology, and Joseph C. Morreale, vice provost for planning, assessment, and research and professor of public administration, Pace University. (90pp, March 1997)

#13: Employment Practices in the Professions: Fresh Ideas From Inside and Outside the Academy #FR13WP

Explores employment arrangements in other professions such as law, medicine, and management and in think-tanks, to ascertain whether policies and practices in these settings have applicability and hold promise for higher education. By C. Ann Trower, senior researcher, Harvard University, Graduate School of Education. (72pp, September 1998)

#14: Alternatives to Tenure for the Next Generation of Academics #FR14WP

Helps answer the question, "What, if anything, would induce individual faculty to renounce tenure?" Develops approaches that could be used to understand the financial value that faculty assign to tenure and the relative appeal of various inducements to forego tenure. By David W. Breneman, professor and dean of education, University of Virginia. (24pp, April 1997)